For Amani and Amelia. For my Black girls.
Love to Laurencio, Ma, Daddy, and Hollis—*JCO*

For Zuri and Sammi, two beautiful Black girls who shine
so brightly. Lots of love from your older cousin!—*BB*

W

PENGUIN WORKSHOP
An imprint of Penguin Random House LLC
1745 Broadway, New York, NY 10019
penguinrandomhouse.com

Text copyright © 2026 by Jaylene Clark Owens
Illustrations copyright © 2026 by Brittney Bond

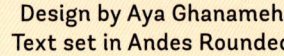

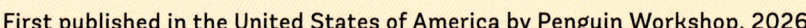

Design by Aya Ghanameh
Text set in Andes Rounded

The art was human made using an iPad Pro and Procreate,
along with Photoshop for further color adjustments.

Library of Congress Cataloging-in-Publication Data is available.

First published in the United States of America by Penguin Workshop, 2026

Manufactured in China
HH

ISBN 9780593889732
10 9 8 7 6 5 4 3 2 1

The authorized representative in the EU for product safety and compliance is Penguin Random House Ireland, Morrison Chambers, 32 Nassau Street, Dublin D02 YH68, Ireland, https://eu-contact.penguin.ie.

A BLACK GIRL and HER BRAIDS

by Jaylene Clark Owens

illustrated by Brittney Bond

Penguin Workshop

A Black girl and her braids
A Black girl and her braids
Can't tell her nothin'
Please don't touch it
You know she looks amaz'

A Black girl and her braids
A Black girl and her braids
Protective style for a while
It's one that always slays

A Black girl and her braids be the best.
When you see her with the fresh plaits,
Know that she is blessed.

No stress from having to do her hair
with the rising of the sun,
    She can just grab a scrunchie,
throw her box braids up into a bun,
    And go!

Or no—
Braids swinging free is a look, too, honey—
Whether they stop at her shoulders, back, or go down to her tummy.

It's a hairstyle that's tried and tested.
It never fails because a Black girl and braids goes best with . . .

Everything!
Sneakers and T-shirts?
Yes!

Pigtails and jean skirts?
The best!

Braids can fulfill all your needs.
And they're even prettier with clips, barrettes, or beads.

But sometimes we're told
that braids are not cool.
That they don't fit in,
that they shouldn't be worn at school.

PROHIBITED HAIRSTYLES
BRAIDS
CORNROWS
TWISTS
AFROS
LOCS
LIVE
NEWS

But braids are not bad,
They're just different from other styles you might see.
And they should be accepted everywhere, just like me!

My braids are special, they are part of my crown,
Of my culture, of my neighborhood, of my family background.

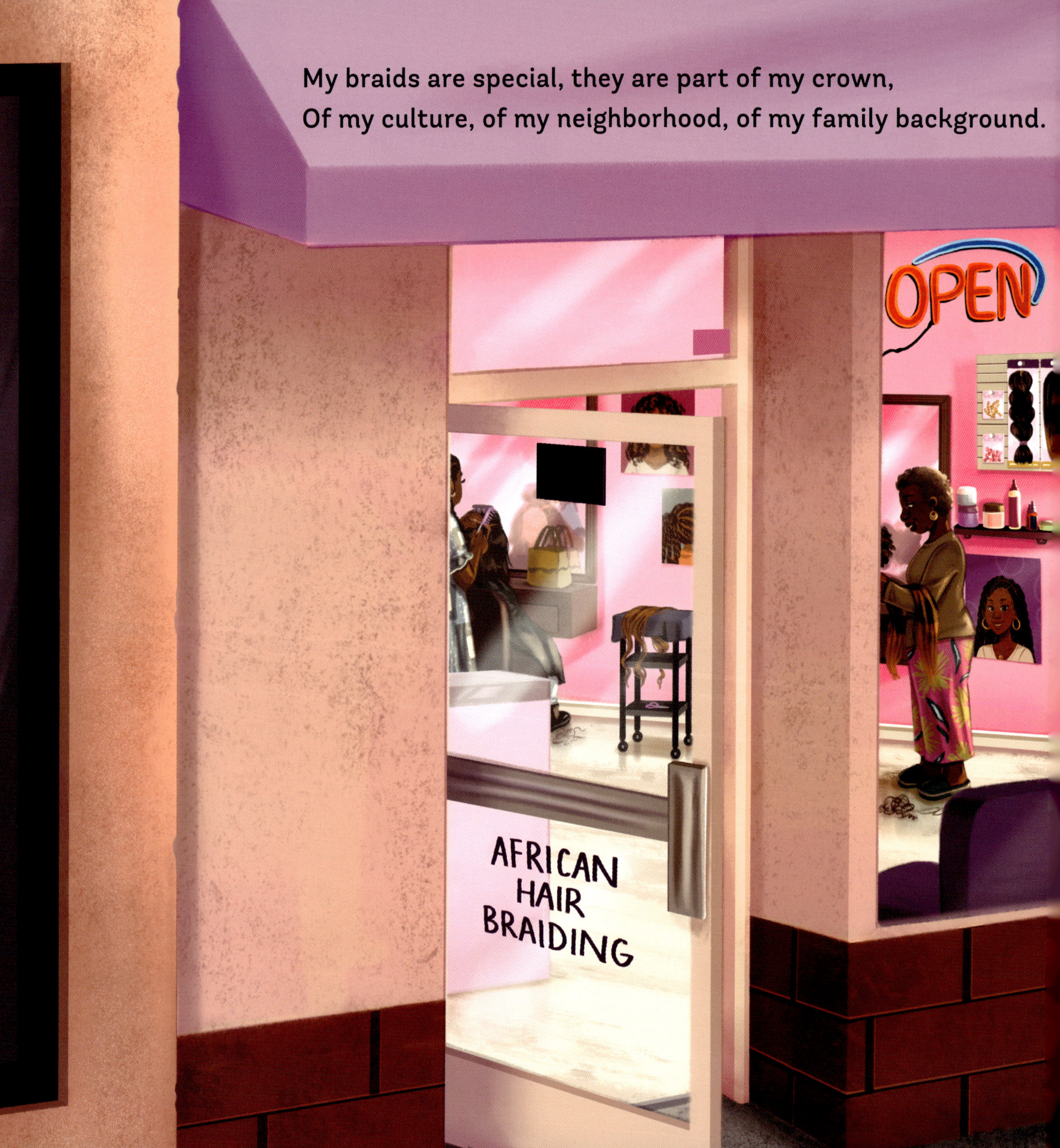

And not just that, they protect my hair—

I can wear them in the rain,
in the pool, I can wear them anywhere!

NO
BRAIDS
TWISTS
AFROS
LOCS

At my best friend's school,
she can't wear braids, twists,
big afros, or locs . . .

My mommy says when I have braids sometimes people put me in a box.
Like a cardboard one with a sign that screams, "Bad Hair!"
But our hair is unique, and special, so that isn't fair!

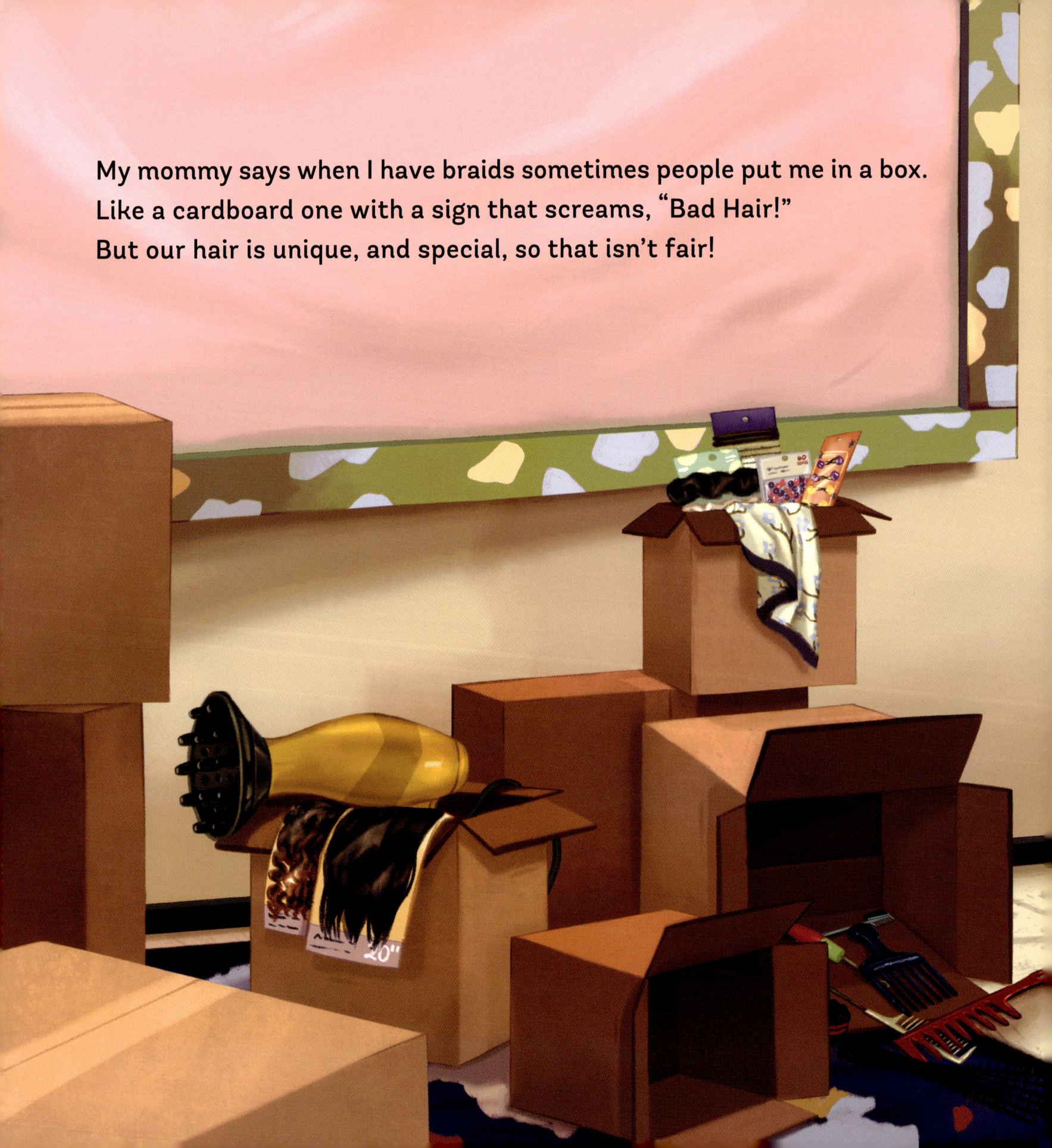

My hair can be in box braids, but the box doesn't belong on me.
A Black girl and her braids—the definition of free!

Even though sometimes my mom has to pay a high price,
She says it's worth it because with braids I feel so nice.

Feels like Christmas,
'cause these braids are a gift,

Swinging them back and forth,
dancing braids are never stiff.

Feels so good when I step out the shop with a fresh set of knotless,

Space buns, cornrows, or maybe even goddess.

Pinned up for a wedding or a ponytail for graduation,
We gon' get it braided up for any occasion.
Rooted in Africa, it's a style that never fades,

Ain't nothin' in this world like a Black girl and her braids!

2 04